TURKEY

by Joanna J. Robinson

The Child's World®

Published by The Child's World®
1980 Lookout Drive • Mankato, MN 56003-1705
800-599-READ • www.childsworld.com

Acknowledgments
The Child's World®: Mary Berendes, Publishing Director
Red Line Editorial: Editorial direction
The Design Lab: Design
Amnet: Production

Design element: Shutterstock Images
Photographs ©: Shutterstock Images, cover (left top),
cover (left center), cover (left bottom), cover (right), 1 (top),
1 (bottom left), 1 (bottom right), 5, 10, 13, 15, 16 (left),
16 (right), 18, 20, 21, 25, 30; Luciano Mortula/
Shutterstock Images, 6–7; Evren Kalinbacak/iStockphoto,
8, 24; Sadik Gulec/Shutterstock Images, 11; iStockphoto,
12, 22, 26; Mehmet Cetin/Shutterstock Images, 17; Fuse/
Thinkstock, 28; Darren Hubley/Shutterstock images, 29

ISBN 9781634070584
LCCN 2014959747

Printed in the United States of America
Mankato, MN
July, 2015
PA02268

ABOUT THE AUTHOR

Joanna J. Robinson is a creative educational writer. She has a passion for providing fun learning materials for children of all ages. Robinson has written educational content and more than 100 original stories. Trips to Mexico, Italy, England, Canada, and Egypt inspire Robinson to share her experiences with young readers.

ONE WORLD · MANY COUNTRIES

TÜRKİYE
20
İSTANBUL

TABLE OF CONTENTS

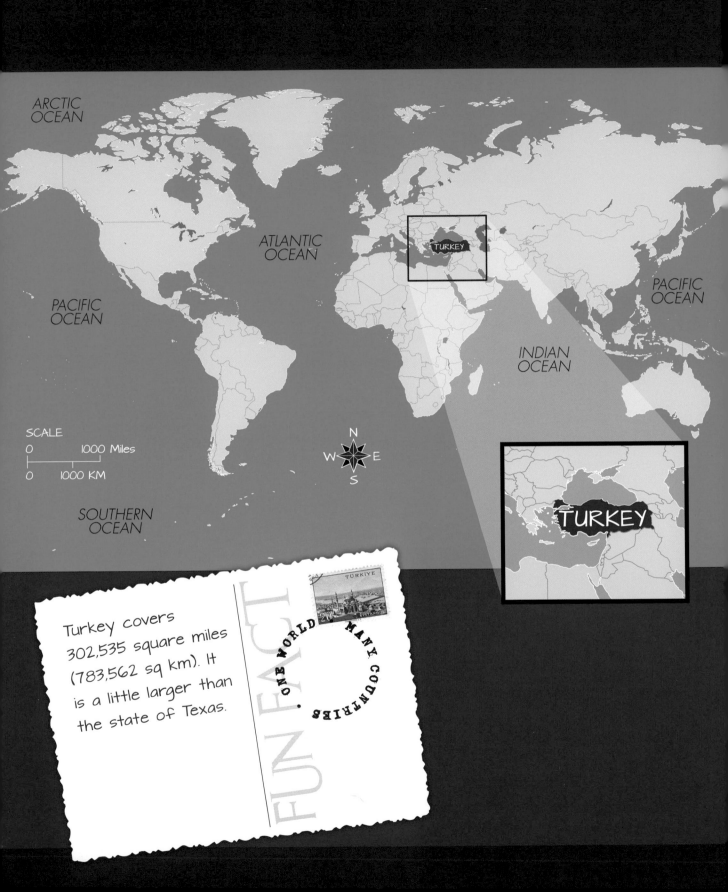

ARCTIC
OCEAN

ATLANTIC
OCEAN

PACIFIC
OCEAN

TURKEY

PACIFIC
OCEAN

INDIAN
OCEAN

SCALE

0   1000 Miles

0   1000 KM

N
W E
S

SOUTHERN
OCEAN

TURKEY

TÜRKİYE
20 İSTANBUL

FUN FACT · ONE WORLD MANY COUNTRIES

Turkey covers
302,535 square miles
(783,562 sq km). It
is a little larger than
the state of Texas.

CHAPTER 1

WELCOME TO TURKEY!

Traditional Turkish carpets line the stalls. No two rugs are exactly alike. Other stalls display colorful fabrics, scarves, and skirts. Nearby, jewelry glitters in its glass case. The smells of leather and spices fill the air. Globe-shaped glass lights hang from the ceiling.

Every inch of every stall is filled. Hand-painted ceramic bowls are carefully stacked. Fabrics are folded neatly. Everything is in its place. Shoppers pack the walkways, searching for deals.

Shoppers look at the stalls in the Grand Bazaar. It is the oldest covered market in the world.

This is the Grand Bazaar in Istanbul, Turkey. It is an amazing place to shop. It is known for its great variety of goods. There are more than 3,000 shops inside. The building has two **mosques**, four fountains, cafés, and restaurants.

The Grand Bazaar reflects the culture that Turkish people have created over many years. It is a blend of religions, languages, and people. Turks have pride in their country's history.

The stalls in the Grand Bazaar are filled with colorful goods, such as ceramic bowls and plates.

CHAPTER 2

THE LAND

↖ Turkey's rocky shore along the Black Sea

Turkey is a **peninsula**. It is the only country that belongs to two continents. Western Turkey is in Europe. Eastern Turkey is in Asia. Turkey serves as a bridge between the two continents.

Along its European border, Turkey has only two neighbors. They are Greece and Bulgaria. On its Asian border, Turkey has five neighbors. They are Syria, Iraq, Iran, Armenia, and Georgia.

Mountains cover most of Turkey's land. Mount Ararat is the highest point in Turkey. It is 16,948 feet (5,166 m) tall. This mountain is an inactive volcano. Some people believe the mountain is **sacred**.

To its north, Turkey borders the Black Sea. The land along the coast is steep and rocky. Thick forests of oak, beech, and elm trees grow in this part of Turkey. This area is also home to the Zonguldak coal mine. It is the largest coal mine in the region.

To its west, Turkey borders the Aegean Sea. Many of Turkey's major rivers flow through this land and into the sea. Many Turks live in the river valleys, where the soil is rich.

The Duden Waterfalls in Antayla, Turkey, flow into the Mediterranean Sea.

Farmers grow crops such as cotton, olives, and figs. Along the coast are beaches and islands.

The Mediterranean Sea is to the south of Turkey. It is known for its beautiful beaches. People from all over the world travel there to enjoy the clear, warm water. This area also has many waterfalls. They splash down cliffs along the coast and into the Mediterranean Sea.

Earthquakes cause major damage in Turkey. These homes in Yalova, Turkey, were destroyed in just 37 seconds during a strong earthquake in 1999.

The climate of Turkey varies. Along the coasts, summers are hot and winters are mild. The coasts receive the most rain. Central Turkey has hot, dry summers. It has very cold winters. Eastern Turkey has short summers and snowy, cold winters. Southeast Turkey has mild, rainy winters.

Earthquakes are common in Turkey. That is because Turkey sits on two major **faults**. As pressure from the earth builds along the faults, the earth moves. This creates earthquakes. About 96 percent of Turkey is at high risk for earthquakes.

Turkey's land is full of natural resources. Turkish mines have coal, copper, and gold. Turkey also has gas and oil reserves. Turkey trades oil and gas with other countries.

FUN FACT

Lake Van is the largest lake in Turkey. This area is home to a type of cat called the Van Kedisi. It is a white cat that has two different colored eyes.

ONE WORLD MANY COUNTRIES

CHAPTER 3

GOVERNMENT AND CITIES

Turkey's official name is the Republic of Turkey. It has 81 provinces. These are smaller divisions in the country, similar to states. Each province has a governor for its leader.

Ankara is home to more than 4 million people.

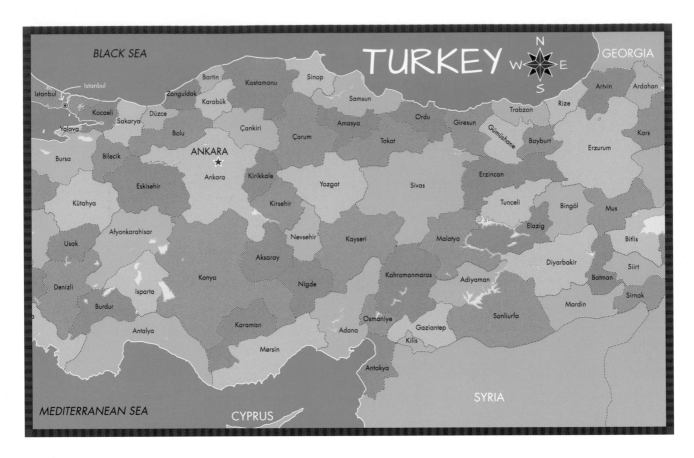

Turkey's national government is a Republican Parliamentary Democracy. In this type of government, Turkish people vote for the president. The president chooses the prime minister. The president and prime minister work with parliament. Members of parliament make Turkey's laws.

Turkey's government meets in the city of Ankara. It is Turkey's capital. Ankara is located on the Ankara River, near the center of Turkey. Its central location makes it an important city for trade. Goods can easily come in and out of the city.

Ankara is home to many of Turkey's businesses. People who live there make tractors, cement, medicines, flour, and fabric.

The fabric from this part of Turkey is known throughout the world. It is made from Angora wool, or mohair. The wool comes from long-haired goats that live near Ankara.

To the west of Ankara is Turkey's largest city, Istanbul. About 11 million people live in Istanbul. It is located where Europe and Asia meet. For the past 2,500 years it has been a place where cultures from Europe and Asia have blended together.

The wool made from Angora goats is soft and fuzzy.

Today, Istanbul remains a powerful and important city. It is Turkey's largest port, and the center of the country's businesses. Istanbul also attracts tourists, who like to look at the city's ancient buildings. One of the most famous is the Hagia Sophia. It began as a Christian church, and was later turned into a mosque.

Istanbul is also an important manufacturing city. Factories produce goods such as chemicals, food, clothing, and shoes. These goods, along with those made in other parts of Turkey,

Turkey's currency

Turkey's flag

The Hagia Sophia was completed in 537 AD.

are important for trade. Turkey **exports** these goods to Germany, Iraq, and Iran.

Turkey **imports** products, too. Some of the imports are machines for Turkey's factories. Turkey also imports oil, cars, clothing, and jewelry. Most of Turkey's imports come from Russia, Germany, and China.

Hazelnuts are an important export for Turkey. Its Black Sea region produces 80 percent of the world's hazelnuts.

FUN FACT

ONE WORLD • MANY COUNTRIES

GLOBAL CONNECTIONS

On August 17, 1999, Turkey had a major earthquake. It was a magnitude 7.6, and it destroyed thousands of homes and businesses. It also took many lives. More than 17,000 Turks died.

This disaster brought the world together. Greece, the United States, France, Mexico, Russia, and Israel sent rescue workers to Turkey. They also sent dogs trained to find people in the rubble. Clothing, tents, blankets, and medical supplies quickly arrived in Turkey.

Life slowly returned to normal for the people of Turkey. They did not want to suffer anything like that again. They could not stop another earthquake, but they could be better prepared.

Engineers designed buildings to be more stable during earthquakes. Volunteers trained Turks on what to do during an earthquake. In schools, children received lessons on earthquake safety.

These actions have made Turkey a world leader in earthquake safety. Today, Turkey's leaders share their knowledge about preparing for earthquakes with other countries throughout the world.

PEOPLE AND CULTURES

A woman in Cappadocia, Turkey, weaves a large carpet. She follows the pattern on her loom to make sure the design comes out correctly.

About 81 million people live in Turkey. Many speak Turkish. Others speak Kurdish. The main religion is Islam. There are also small groups of Christians and Jews.

Mevlevi dancers spin as they dance.

Turkish people have many traditions. One tradition is rug weaving. The rugs are made from the finest wool, silk, or cotton. Weavers use traditional designs on the rugs, such as flowers, leaves, and trees. These rugs are in demand in many parts of the world.

Turkey also has special dances. Mevlevi dancers perform a dance that is a form of prayer. The dancers are called whirling dervishes. They spin on one foot as they circle the room. A dancer's right hand faces heaven. The left hand faces Earth. The dancers represent Earth spinning around the sun.

Turkish people celebrate Republic Day on October 29. On that day in 1923, Turkish leaders declared Turkey's independence from the **Ottoman Empire**. Today, people celebrate by going to parades and watching fireworks. Schools have special performances, and Turkish leaders give speeches.

Ramadan is a Muslim holiday celebrated in Turkey. Ramadan lasts for one month. During this month, most Muslims **fast**. They do not eat between sunrise and sunset.

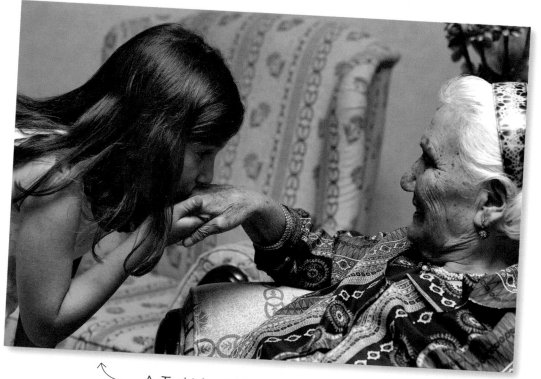

A Turkish girl kisses her grandmother's hand as part of the Sugar Festival after Ramadan.

People are only allowed to eat at certain times during Ramadan. The *suhoor* meal is served before sunrise. The *iftar* meal is served after sunset. Meals include fruits, vegetables, meats, and cheeses.

The month of Ramadan ends with a three-day Sugar Festival. People can eat sweets again. Children wear their best clothes and go door-to-door. They kiss each adult's hands to show respect. They get sweets and money in return.

April 23 is Children's Day in Turkey. On that day, children pretend to elect a president and run the government. They also decorate lanterns. The lanterns represent how children light up the future.

FUN FACT

ONE WORLD • MANY COUNTRIES

CHAPTER 5

DAILY LIFE

Traditional Turkish homes

In Turkey, most people live in cities. They make their homes in modern apartment buildings made out of concrete. Apartments usually have common walls with neighbors on each side.

Outside of the city, Turkey still has many traditional homes. They are built from wood, brick, and stone. The homes are often two stories tall. In the past, each room in the home could serve many purposes. It was possible to cook, eat, sleep, read, and worship all in the same room. The items for each activity were stored in cupboards and taken out as needed.

To get from place to place, people in Turkey have many choices. Some cities have trams that take people where they need to go. For longer distances, people travel by bus or car. Along the coast, boats carry people to and from islands.

Every day 5 million people in Istanbul use public transportation, including trams.

A Turkish woman wears a traditional headscarf.

In Turkey many people dress in clothing similar to that worn in the United States. Some people also choose to wear traditional clothing. Men wear baggy pants with a wide belt and a loose shirt. Women's traditional clothing includes a skirt, shirt, and apron.

Head coverings were are also part of traditional Turkish clothing. Many men wore a fez, which is a tall hat with a tassel. Some men also wore turbans, which were long pieces of cloth wrapped around the head. Women wore scarves over their heads.

In 1925, Turkey's leader Mustafa Kemal Atatürk outlawed fez, turbans, and headscarves. The head coverings were a symbol of people who practiced Islam. Atatürk wanted to make Turkey a modern, **secular** nation. The head coverings did not fit with his modern ideas.

Today, Atatürk's laws are still in place. They are slowly changing, though. Recently, Turkey wrote a new dress code for schools. Now, girls are allowed to wear headscarves once again. Women who work in government offices are also allowed to wear them.

Turkish food is mix of many flavors. It has been influenced by its neighbors in Asia and Europe. Many dishes include lamb, eggplant, and yogurt. Rice is common. For dessert, many Turks enjoy *baklava*. It is a flaky pastry with honey and nuts. Candy made with rose petals is also popular. It is called Turkish delight, or *lokum*.

Many families eat their meals together in Turkey.

Turkey's food, clothing, and homes are a mix of many cultures. They have been influenced from Asia and Europe. The Turkish people are proud of this blend of culture they have created.

DAILY LIFE FOR CHILDREN

Turkish children attend school. They study subjects such as math, science, and reading. In fourth grade, students learn a foreign language. Fifth-grade students can begin trade school.

After school, children do homework and play with friends. Shooting marbles is a popular way to pass the afternoon. Children also like to play *korebe*. It is a game of blindfolded tag.

Families eat dinner late. Children play games or watch television in the evening. Many go to bed around 10:00 at night.

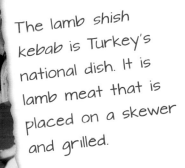

The lamb shish kebab is Turkey's national dish. It is lamb meat that is placed on a skewer and grilled.

FUN FACT

ONE WORLD · MANY COUNTRIES

TÜRKIYE

FAST FACTS

Population: 82 million

Area: 302,535 square miles (783,562 sq km)

Capital: Ankara

Largest Cities: Istanbul, Ankara, and Izmir

Form of Government: Republican Parliamentary Democracy

Language: Turkish

Trading Partners:
Germany, Iraq, and Russia

Major Holidays:
Ramadan, Republic Day, and
Children's Day

National Dish: *Shish kebab* (grilled lamb meat on a skewer), served with vegetables and rice

Turkish students often wear uniforms to school.

GLOSSARY

exports (ek-SPORTS) When a country exports goods, it is selling them to other countries. Turkey exports goods to other countries.

fast (FAST) To fast is to go without eating. People in Turkey fast during Ramadan.

faults (falts) Faults are places where the earth's crust is split. Turkey sits on two faults.

imports (ihm-PORTS) When a country imports goods, it buys them from other countries. Turkey imports many goods.

mosques (MOSKS) Mosques are Muslim places of worship. People go to mosques to pray.

Ottoman Empire (AH-tuh-mun EM-pire) The Ottoman Empire was one of the world's most powerful empires in the 1500s until the 1920s. It included Turkey and many other countries.

peninsula (puh-NIN-suh-luh) A peninsula is a piece of land that is almost entirely surrounded by water. Turkey is a peninsula.

sacred (SAY-krid) Sacred describes something that is holy, loved, and respected. Some people believe Mount Ararat is sacred.

secular (se-KYU-lar) Secular describes something that is controlled by the government and not a church. Turkey is a secular country.

To Learn More

BOOKS

Jackson, Elaine. *Discover Turkey*. New York: PowerKids Press, 2012.

Macaulay, David. *Mosque*. Boston, MA: Houghton Mifflin Co., 2003.

Shields, Sarah. *National Geographic Countries of the World: Turkey*. Washington, D.C.: National Geographic Society, 2009.

WEB SITES

Visit our Web site for links about Turkey: childsworld.com/links

Note to Parents, Teachers, and Librarians: We routinely verify our Web links to make sure they are safe and active sites. So encourage your readers to check them out!

Index